Math

Right From the Start

What Parents Can Do in the
First Five Years

Teaching
Strategies® Inc.
Washington, DC

As of this printing, the books listed on pages 54-56 are in print. The publisher cannot guarantee how long they will remain in print.

Interior illustrations: Anthony Alex LeTourneau
Cover, book design, layout, and production: Abner Nieves

First edition 2008

Teaching Strategies, Inc.
P.O. Box 42243
Washington, DC 20015
www.TeachingStrategies.com

ISBN: 978-1-879537-98-9

Library of Congress Control Number: 2008923450

14 13 12 11 10 09 08   1 2 3 4 5 6 7 8

Table of Contents

Introduction

Are you the parent, relative, or caregiver of a baby, toddler, or preschool child?

What do you think of when you hear the word *math*? Numbers and counting? Adding and subtracting? Something you are good at—or not good at?

Many people think math is counting and recognizing numbers. But *mathematics* is so much more! It is a way of seeing how things are the same and different. It is a way to organize information. It is a way to understand quantity (how much), numbers, patterns, space, and shapes. Mathematics gives us a sense of order, a way to predict things, compare things, and solve problems. Mathematics is everywhere! And it is already a part of your child's world. In fact, research shows that young children are born with an informal understanding of math.

Do you want your child to

- enjoy math?

- feel good about her math skills?

- use math to figure things out and solve problems?

- succeed in school and in life?

You can see how your child uses math to make sense of the world. Your baby learns the difference between adults she knows and adults she doesn't know. Your 1-year-old asks for more cookies and cries when someone takes one away. Your 2-year-old holds up two fingers to show how old he is. Your 3-year-old shows what she knows about shapes and space when she turns and stacks blocks to make a tower. Your 4-year-old picks out patterns in the bathroom floor tiles. And your 5-year-old loves to tell you how tall she is and how she keeps getting taller!

Math is a big part of our everyday life. When you sort laundry and match socks, you're using math. When you set the table for a meal and make sure each person has a plate, knife, fork, and glass, you're using math. When you keep score or time at a basketball or football game, you're using math. And when you use maps to get from one place to another or give a friend directions to get somewhere, you're also using math!

Your child uses math when he plays and when he helps you do things like put toys away and cook. All day long, there are many chances for "math talk" and "math play" with your child. You don't need to buy special games or toys. You don't even have to be good at math to support math learning. This book shows you how you can support your child's natural interest in math and help him learn and use math skills during everyday experiences. You'll see how much you already do. You'll learn new ideas to try. Choose the ones you and your child will enjoy the most. And have fun!

What Is Mathematics?

You may think it's hard to help your child learn and use math skills. You may not have had good experiences with math when you were in school. But don't be afraid! You can introduce basic math ideas to your child in ways that are meaningful and fun.

Here is information about five areas of math. It will help you notice times during the day for math talk and math play.

Numbers

We use numbers to help us talk about amounts. Children who have a sense of number understand how numbers are used and how number concepts are related.

Knowing about numbers:

- Count by saying numbers in a certain order, match each number with one of the items being counted.

- Figure out how many objects are in a group.

- Compare groups and figuring out which ones have more, fewer, or less.

- Understand order (first, second, and third).

- Explore written numbers.

- Put groups of things together to find out how many in all.

- Take something away from a group and find out how many are left.

- Have a group of things and share them by making smaller groups.

- Make equal groups of things to give out.

Geometry
(shapes and space)

Geometry involves shape, size, space, position, direction, and movement. Having a sense of space means knowing where you are in relation to people and objects around you.

Knowing about shapes and space:

- Recognize shapes such as circles, squares, rectangles, cubes, and cylinders; build with shapes; describe shapes; compare shapes; and sort shapes.

- Describe shapes and other objects using location and position words such as *on, off, under, below, in, out, right,* and *left* and distance words such as *near, far,* and *next to.*

- Move shapes by sliding them to a new position, flipping them over, turning them, or combining them.

Measurement

Measuring involves comparing and figuring out how long or short something is, how much something weighs, or how much time it takes to do something. When young children say things like "I'm bigger than you" and "This rock is fat … I can't move it," they are using comparing and measuring language.

Knowing about measuring:

- Describe how long or tall something is; how much something holds; how heavy something is; how much space is covered; and how long it takes to get somewhere.

- Compare two objects by specific features; compare three or more objects or events and put them in order.

- Choose the right tool to measure something.

Patterns and Change

Understanding patterns is a building block for understanding algebra. Change is also an important idea for young children to understand. Understanding change means learning that things change over time and that change can be described using math words. Learning about patterns and change helps children think in creative ways.

Patterns are formed when objects, events, or sounds are repeated a number of times. Figuring out a pattern involves seeing relationships that make up the pattern. It might be a pattern of sizes (large, small; large, small). It could be a pattern of colors (red, blue; red, blue). Patterns are found in music, such as repeating "E-I-E-I-O" in "Old MacDonald Had a Farm." They are also found in daily events (for example, "After my cereal, I get my bottle.").

Knowing about patterns and change:

- Recognize and make patterns that repeat, such as patterns of size, color, shape, and rhythm.

- Recognize patterns that grow, such as staircases and songs that add one word or action to each verse.

- Recognize and talk about change using words such as *smaller, bigger,* and *fuller* and numbers, such as changing a shirt size from 7 to 8.

Collecting and Organizing Information

This part of math involves collecting, organizing, and presenting information in ways that make sense.

Knowing about collecting and organizing information:

- Recognize how objects are the same and different.

- Separate objects into groups by features, such as size, color, shape, sound, and use.

- Present information using objects, drawings, pictures, charts, and graphs.

- Describe information using words like *more*, *fewer*, *the same as*, *smaller than*, and *not* (as in "The shapes in this group are circles. The shapes in that group are *not* circles.").

How Children Learn

How children learn about math is just as important as *what* children learn. Here are some important ways that you can help your child learn about math:

Talk with your child!

Listen to what your child says to you. Use math words when you describe what you see, hear, and do and what your child sees, hears, and does. Help her find ways to express her ideas with math words, pictures, and symbols. The more math talk your child hears, the better she will get at using math language.

Solve problems together!

Help him learn that there are many ways to solve a problem and that a problem can have more than one answer. What's important for young children is *how* they come to an answer, not just getting the right one. Over time and with a lot of practice, your child can become a great problem solver!

Ask WHY questions!

Ask your child questions such as why she put all the little trucks in one box or matched the blue sock to the white one. Listen to her reasons. Share your ideas. Give your child lots of chances to explain why she thinks as she does or why she makes a choice between one guess and another. Don't worry if the reasons don't make sense. Children don't always know how they get their answers. But that's okay. It's the thinking process that counts.

Draw and write about math!

Help your child share his ideas about math using drawings and objects such as blocks, counters, and fingers. Ask questions and make comments and suggestions, such as "Can you make a drawing …?", "Can you use blocks…?", "Show me what you mean …" and "Tell me more about how…." Remember that children also love to copy what adults do. Show your child how you use tally marks and maps. Share ads that show how much something costs.

Give Your Baby a Good Start

How can my child learn about math? He's just a baby. He's crawling, not walking. He makes sounds, not words. What should I do? What should I say?

Even though your baby may not be walking and talking, there's a lot you can do and say to help him develop and learn! First, think about some of the things your baby learns in his first year of life. He learns to hold his head up, then he turns over. He follows moving objects with his eyes. He finds his feet! He learns to grasp rattles and shake them on purpose. He learns who his family members are and can tell them apart from people who are not family members. He likes some foods and dislikes other foods. He gurgles, coos, babbles, and may make sounds that sound like real words.

And that's just in the first six months or so! Then, he sits up. He crawls and pulls up on furniture to stand. He may even take some steps and begin to walk by the time he is a year old! And he makes a very important discovery: He learns that people and things usually exist even when he can't see them. With these skills and more, your baby is ready to make discoveries about math.

You can help! For example, when you create and follow your baby's daily schedule, you set the stage for helping him learn about patterns. Counting his toes, tickling his tummy, and clapping his hands together help him learn about where he is in relation to objects and people. You help him learn about numbers when you count out loud the objects hanging from his mobile. When you give him interesting objects to play with, he learns about how things are the same and different. And when you talk to him about what he sees and does, and what you see and do, you help him pay attention to the world around him and introduce new math words and ideas.

What might you
see babies do
when they discover
math ideas?

*What might you
do to help your
baby learn?*

Numbers

A young baby might …

- look at you closely as you put on her socks and say, "Here's one sock for this foot, and one sock for your other foot. Two feet, two socks."

- smile when you bring her more cereal and ask, "Do you want *more* cereal? You must be hungry!"

An older baby might …

- place a lid on each container with which he is playing.

- reach for more toys.

- make a sign for *more* after finishing a cracker.

What you can do and say

Count everything!
Point to or touch each object as you say the number name.

This helps your baby
Hear number names.
Learn that one number goes with each object counted.

Describe what your baby sees or does.
"Here's *one* mitten for this hand, and *one* mitten for your other hand. *Two* hands, *two* mittens."
"That's the *third* time you've rolled over today. You rolled over *three* times!"
"You're reaching toward the blocks. Do you want *more* blocks?"

This helps your baby
Hear words for number, order, and quantity (how much).

Read number books with your baby.

This helps your baby
Learn number names.
Connect books with feeling safe and happy in your lap.

Give your baby toys such as nesting cups and stacking rings. Describe what your baby does, "You put the *smaller* cup inside the *larger* cup!" Ask questions, such as "How will you get that *little* ring to fit on the stack?"

This helps your baby
Explore different sizes.
Hear words that describe or compare sizes.

Play peek-a-boo.

This helps your baby
Learn that objects and people exist even when he can't see them.

Geometry
(Shapes and Space)

A young baby might ...

- place his hands around a bottle, feeling its shape.

- experience being wrapped in a blanket.

- run her hands back and forth along the edge of a table.

An older baby might ...

- crawl through a tunnel and enjoy the feeling of being in a space where she can see out both ends.

- bang blocks against different slots in a shape-sorting box until they fall through.

- drop a ball into a basket.

What you can do and say

Play body games such as "Pat-a-Cake" and "This Little Piggy."

> **This helps your baby**
> > Become aware of her body and learn where her
> > body parts are.
> > Become aware of where she is in relation to people and
> > objects around her.

Move to a beat with your baby. Dance with him in your arms.
Gently bounce him on your knee. If he's standing or walking, hold
his hands while you dance together.

> **This helps your baby**
> > Learn about his position in space.

Let your baby crawl *in* and *out* and *over* and *under* objects such as
cardboard boxes, tunnels, and floor pillows.

> **This helps your baby**
> > Experience different positions in space such as *inside,*
> > *outside, over,* and *under.*

Describe what your baby sees and does:
> "Your arms go *in* the shirt sleeves. Your legs go *in* the pants.
> And your hat goes *on* your head!"
> "You are sitting *next to* Nana."
> "That orange looks like a *ball.*"
> "Uh, oh, your *ball* rolled *under* the table. How can you get it?"

> **This helps your baby**
> > Hear words that describe position and location.
> > Learn the names of shapes.

Let your baby explore books about shapes and toys that have
interesting shapes. As he looks at pictures in the books and plays
with the toys, say the names of the shapes and describe them.

> **This helps your baby**
> > Learn that some objects are like other objects.
> > Learn the names of shapes.

Patterns

A young baby might ...

- focus on the color or texture of your clothes.

- wave her arms when she sees you come with her bottle.

- stroke a rough carpet; feel the smooth tile floor.

An older baby might ...

- open his mouth when you lift a spoon toward his face.

- play with nesting cups, trying out different sizes until she finds one that fits inside another.

- place a few small blocks in a line, spread them around the floor, and then collect and line them up again.

What you can do and say

Try to do everyday routines and activities in the same way or in the same order each day.

This helps your baby
Learn what to expect.
Feel a sense of order and feel secure.

Sing songs and lullabies that have words or phrases that repeat.

This helps your baby
Experience patterns in songs.

Describe what your baby sees, and does:
"Look at the stripes on your shirt: a red stripe, and then a yellow one. Red, and then yellow again."
"It's nap time. I'll read your favorite book and sing your favorite song to help you fall asleep."
"Every time I pick up your spoon and give it to you, you drop it on the ground. I pick it up, you drop it again. You must like this game!"

This helps your baby
Learn about different kinds of patterns.

Give your baby small, soft blocks. Describe the *size*, *shape*, and *color* of the blocks. Describe what your baby does with them.

This helps your baby
Explore objects and see how they are the *same* and *different*.

Sorting and Classifying

(Beginning skills for measuring, collecting, and organizing information)

....

A young baby might ...

- recognize your voice when he hears you say, "I'm coming. I hear you calling me."

- tell the difference between adults she knows and adults she doesn't know.

- show a liking for a certain soft blanket and enjoy stroking it.

An older baby might ...

- hit a drum with a wooden stick but shake a rattle.

- pick out all the orange pieces from a fruit salad.

- collect wooden blocks and put them in a box.

What you can do and say

Arrange your baby's clothes, toys, and diapering supplies. Talk with him about how things go together, "Let's put your baby dolls on the bottom shelf and your books in the basket," or "Which ones are your bath toys?"

This helps your baby
Learn how things that are the same go together.

Describe what your baby sees and does:
"You always smile when Daddy picks you up!"
"You like eating peaches, but you make a face when I give you applesauce."
"When you shake the rattle with the bells inside, it makes a soft tinkling sound. When you shake the plastic keys, they make a loud clacking sound."
"The smooth ball rolls when you push it, but the bumpy ball doesn't."

This helps your baby
Become aware that things can be grouped.

Let your baby play with things that fit together. Look for things around the house such as round objects that fit in cupcake pans and different size pots and boxes with matching lids.

This helps your baby
Explore matching sizes and shapes.

Your Baby Learns All Day Long

What's a baby's day like? Much of it is spent being diapered, dressed, fed, and bathed, and taking naps. Part of it may include saying goodbye when you leave her at child care and hello when you come together again. That means your baby's busy day is your busy day, too. It may seem like there's no time to do anything extra in between these daily routines. But those are perfect times to bond with your baby and introduce her to math ideas.

Very young children learn through the trusting relationships they build with the important adults in their lives. That means you! Every daily routine gives you a chance to talk and play with your baby. The one-on-one time you spend helps your baby learn to trust and feel safe with you. As your baby learns new skills and takes part more and more in daily routines, he develops a sense of all the things he can do. Every routine becomes a time to support your baby's interest in his world and guide him in learning more about it.

So while you diaper, bathe, feed, and dress your baby, talk to him. Use math words and ask questions to develop his math thinking. Don't worry if your baby doesn't understand what you say. He still learns from the tone of your voice and the expressions on your face. Over time, your baby will get used to hearing your language and begin to learn what the words mean.

Give Your Toddler a Good Start

My toddler is a bundle of energy. She doesn't sit still! She walks, runs, and gets into everything. I can barely keep up with making sure she doesn't hurt herself. How can I possibly find time to teach her math?

Toddlers are always be on the move. But this is a great time for your toddler to learn about many things, including math. The world is an exciting place and she has many more skills with which to explore it. She can talk with you using gestures like pointing, saying words, and even speaking in simple sentences. She can use her fingers and hands to put puzzle pieces in place, make marks with a crayon, and string large beads to make necklaces. She can walk and run with greater ease and learn to hop, throw a ball, and climb.

Your toddler is also gaining important thinking skills. She better understands that people and things exist even when she can't see them. She begins to understand basic ideas about time and to recognize there is an order to daily events. She can compare groups of things using the words *more* and *same*. She begins to sort objects by size, shape, color, and how they feel. She begins to solve problems involving space as she fills containers and dumps things out. And she starts to explore her world through pretend play. Pretending is an important skill. When your toddler holds a block to her ear like a phone or pretends to feed a doll, it means she can hold a picture of something in her mind. And it means she can use one object to stand for something else. This is called *abstract thinking*. Abstract thinking is needed for learning to read and for math.

What might you see toddlers do when they discover math ideas?

What might you do to help your toddler learn?

Numbers

A toddler might …

- stomp around the room, singing, "One, two, one, two, five!"

- help you put a napkin on each plate when you set the table.

- notice that another child has a larger lump of clay and ask you for more.

A 2-year-old might …

- line up toy cars and place one block next to each car.

- build a tower with blocks and say, "Mine bigger."

- hold up two fingers when you ask, "How old are you?" and say, "I two."

What you can do and say

Keep counting with your child! Count the steps he climbs; food you put in a grocery cart; the blocks he uses to build a tower; and the number of times you push him on a swing.

> **This helps your toddler**
> Learn number names.
> Learn that one number goes with each object counted.
> Learn to count in a particular order.

Describe what your toddler sees or does.
"You picked out the *biggest* ball!"
"You had *two* apple slices and you ate *one*. Now you only have *one* slice."
"Let's see how many trucks you have. *One, two, three. Three* trucks!"
"You have *two* dolls and I have *two* dolls. We both have the *same* number of dolls!"

> **This helps your toddler**
> Learn words for numbers, order, and quantity (how much).
> Learn about size and how to compare amounts.

Read or tell stories that include numbers.

> **This helps your toddler**
> Learn number names.

Let your toddler play with empty food containers, milk cartons, and boxes that fit one into another.

> **This helps your toddler**
> Explore different sizes.
> Learn about how objects relate to each other.

Say rhymes and sing songs and fingerplays that use numbers, such as "One, two, buckle my shoe," and "1-2-3-4-5, I caught a fish alive."

> **This helps your toddler**
> Learn about numbers and counting.

Geometry
(Shapes and Space)

....

A toddler might ...

- try to put a teddy bear into a box that is too small; then find a larger box and put the bear into it.

- know whether to go *around, in,* or *through* a structure to get to an object or person

- play with different shapes and put all the cubes in a bucket.

A 2-year-old might ...

- blow bubbles outdoors and say, "Look! Balls. Lots of balls!"

- learn the names of some shapes: "This a circle. It's my pizza."

- bend down to look when you say, "Your shoes are under the bed."

What you can do and say

Move and dance together. Give your toddler streamers and scarves to wave while dancing.

> **This helps your toddler**
> Learn about her position in space.

Encourage your toddler to crawl and climb *in* and *out* and *over* and *under* objects such as cardboard boxes, tunnels, and floor pillows. Take her to playgrounds that have low, safe structures to climb.

> **This helps your toddler**
> Pay attention to where objects and spaces are in relation to each other.
> Explore how her body fits in space.

Describe what your toddler sees and does:
"There are lots of *circles* on your shirt."
"That block is shaped like a train car."
"You're hiding *under* the table!"
"You're stacking *cubes*. It looks like you're building a tall tower."

> **This helps your toddler**
> Learn words that describe position and location.
> Learn the names of shapes.

Cut food into different shapes such as toast into triangles and cheese slices into rectangles. Serve round foods like crackers, cucumber slices, or tortillas for snack. Talk about the shapes of the food.

> **This helps your toddler**
> Learn the names of shapes.

Provide materials to build with such as blocks, Duplos®, empty boxes, and milk cartons.

> **This helps your toddler**
> Learn that some objects are like other objects.
> Learn how shapes fit together.

Patterns

A toddler might ...

- beat a drum, imitating the way you do it.

- use a small cup to fill a larger one with sand.

- say a word that is repeated in a storybook while you read it aloud.

A 2-year-old might ...

- line up cars of different sizes, putting the big ones together and the little ones together.

- put all the green cubes in one pile and the yellow cubes in another pile.

- place rings on a stacking toy in order of size.

- beat a drum after hearing you clap your hands.

What you can do and say

Talk about the events of the day: "First we eat breakfast, and then I'll take you to school. After school, I'll pick you up and then we'll come home."

> **This helps your toddler**
> Learn that the order of events is a kind of pattern.

Read books with words and phrases that repeat such as *Brown Bear, Brown Bear, What Do You See?*

> **This helps your toddler**
> Learn about patterns that repeat in a regular way.

Describe what your toddler sees, hears, and does:
  "Look at the flashing lights. The colors keep changing: red, green; red, green; red, green; red, green!"
  "Listen to the bells ringing – two high sounds and a low sound; two high sounds and a low sound; two high sounds and a low sound."
  "You lined up the farm animals: a cow; then a sheep; then another cow; then another sheep; then another cow; and then another sheep."

> **This helps your toddler**
> Learn to recognize different kinds of patterns.

Give your child toys such as colored wooden blocks, large beads and laces, and plastic snap beads. Find objects in your house, such as empty thread spools, plastic spoons and forks, and different sizes and colors of socks. Describe the patterns your child makes. Make a simple pattern using objects, sounds, or movements. Invite your child to make one that looks or sounds like yours.

> **This helps your toddler**
> See, recognize, and repeat relationships that make
>   up patterns.
> Learn number concepts.

Sorting and Classifying

(Beginning skills for measuring, collecting, and organizing information)

. . . .

A toddler might …

- see a picture of a donkey and say, "Horsie."

- place a blue block next to another blue block.

- place blocks of different shapes into the matching holes in a shape-sorter box.

A 2-year-old might …

- put all of the yellow blocks in a bucket.

- pick out all of the cows from a pile of farm animals.

- pick out all of the cubes from a pile of different shapes and then build a tower.

What you can do and say

Invite your toddler to help you clean up and put things where they belong, such as clothes, toys, lids for pots and pans, and so on. Explain how things that are the same go together, "All the socks go in this pile, all the lids go in this drawer."

This helps your toddler
Practice sorting things.
Understand that things can be grouped.

Describe what your toddler sees and does:
"You seem to like the blue playdough best."
"I put your favorite books on this shelf where you can reach them."
"You put all your stuffed animals in the baby carriage."
"Thanks for helping me collect your sippy cups to wash."

This helps your toddler
Learn that things can be grouped by different features.

Give your toddler collections of things that she can group in different ways, such as large plastic bottle caps, plastic animals, pinecones, and shells.

This helps your toddler
See how things are the same and different.
Explore ways to group things together.

Your Toddler Learns All Day Long

The world is an exciting place for toddlers, and they are learning new things every moment of every day. Think about all the things you do with your toddler every day. There are routines like diapering and learning to use the toilet, dressing, napping, bathing, and eating. There are daily activities like shopping, going to the doctor, taking walks and rides, and visiting family and friends.

All of these are great times to build your relationship with your child and to help her learn math ideas and skills. Remember that much of your child's learning comes from just talking to her. When you point out things like numbers, shapes, size, and amounts and describe what she is doing using math words, you help her learn the language of math. Talk about what you are doing as you shop, build things, and cook. Think out loud as you use math to solve problems or explain an idea.

And help your toddler make believe! Make believe, or *pretend play*, is one of the most important ways that children learn about the world and relationships with people. When children make believe, they learn about people, how objects are used, and ways to make things happen. They develop and practice important thinking skills like remembering something they've seen before. They start to use objects to stand for other things such as using a block as a car or telephone. These skills will help children later understand that numbers tell us the amount of something. For example, two can mean that the child has two shoes. They will also use numbers to compare groups of objects.

Try these ideas. Help your toddler learn math and have fun at the same time!

Talk about real life experiences as they take place.

When you take your toddler places like the grocery store, post office, or clinic, talk about what is happening. Explain what people are doing, their jobs, and the names of tools and other objects they use. This helps your toddler understand and remember experiences.

Provide props that inspire pretend play.

Dolls, doll blankets, a cradle, stuffed animals, telephones (toy or real), pots, pans, and plastic dishes are great toys. Other fun props include plastic people and animals; toy cars, trucks, and boats; and ride-on toys. Playing with these toys helps your toddler remember and act out what she's seen. They also help her explore math ideas like counting, size, shape, and sorting and comparing things.

Let your child dress up.

Support your toddler's interest in pretend play by providing dress-up clothes and props such as firefighter hats and work gloves. Dressing up helps your child explore math ideas such as size, shape, and patterns on clothes.

Play make-believe games with your child.

This is one of the best ways to help your toddler pretend. As you play, ask questions. Offer a new prop. Take on a role yourself.

Toddlers are active learners. They look, listen, and do. Your busy toddler will learn math ideas when she has lots of chances to explore and play with interesting things. And she will soak up even more when you take an interest in what she is doing and talk to her about all the new things she's learning!

Give Your Preschool Child a Good Start

My preschool child seems so grown up now! He talks a lot. He notices so many things and asks so many questions, some of which I have a hard time answering! He can do lots of things on his own, and loves to help with anything he can. And he's learning so much at school. So what can I teach him?

Your preschool child is learning a lot at school or child care, but you're still his best and most important teacher! The preschool years can be exciting ones for you and your child. Make the most of them.

Think about all the things children can do when they are 3-, 4-, and 5-years-old. They walk, run, climb up and down steps, jump, and ride a tricycle. They can do things for themselves like wash their hands, brush their teeth, put clothes on, and take them off. Their knowledge and use of language is growing. They can talk about things that happen to them and learn and use new words every day. They can put puzzles with more pieces together, string beads, and put pegs in a pegboard. They start drawing simple shapes. And they build more and more interesting towers and buildings with blocks!

Preschool children are also developing important thinking skills that are related to math learning. For example, as they put together puzzles, they start to understand that a whole object can be separated into parts. As their language skills increase, they compare and talk about objects and shapes. They can describe objects that are the same and different. They learn to count to 10, and begin to recognize written numbers 0 to 9. When counting things in a group, they can label each object with just one number word to figure out how many things they have. Some children can even add and subtract objects using numbers up to four! And children start to recognize shapes such as circle, square, triangle, and rectangle.

What might you see preschool children do when they discover math ideas?

What might you do to help your preschool child learn?

Numbers

- notice that it takes five scoops of sand to fill a cup.

- guess that it will take 10 blocks to make a fence, then count to see if her guess is right.

- count to five and then set the table with five plates, napkins, and forks.

- show he is 4 years old by showing four fingers on his hand.

- answer, "Three!" when given two cookies and asked how many she would have if you gave her one more.

- count, "7, 8, 9, 10, oneteen, twoteen, threeteen."

What you can do and say

Invite your child to count and touch each object with you as you say the number. Count incorrectly sometimes or forget which things you already counted. Ask your child to help you find your mistakes.

This helps your preschool child
Learn that you number each object as you count.
Learn to count in a particular order.
Learn that the last number named when counting a group of objects tells how many are in the group.

Describe what your preschool child sees or does.
"Who has *more* marbles, you or your sister?"
"I have *three* books and you have *one*. How many do we have *all together*?"
"You were the *second* person to come to the table. Nana got here *first*."

This helps your preschool child
Learn words for number and order.
Count groups of things. Compare amounts.

Read counting books. Help your child make a number book.

This helps your preschool child
Learn number names.
Recognize some written numbers.
Learn to match a group of objects with its written number.

Play games with 5 objects and 10 objects. For example, ask your child to toss 5 or 10 pennies. Invite her to count how many land heads-up and how many land heads-down.

This helps your preschool child
Learn about *quantity* (how many are in a group).
Quickly see how many objects are in a group.

Invite your child to tell *how many* stories. For example, she can tell how many rode in the car to the store, how many played in the sandbox, and how many footsteps it took to walk across the room.

This helps your preschool child
Learn about numbers and counting.
Learn about *quantity* (how many are in a group).

Geometry
(Shapes and Space)

A preschool child might …

- say, "You put your horse inside the fence. I'm going to make mine jump over the fence."

- note that bubbles look like circles.

- laugh every time she puts two triangle blocks together and makes a square.

- show his friend how to build a block boat and tell him, "Do it this way. You need a square block like this. No, no, do it like me! You have to turn it over to make it go right."

- use empty boxes and tubes to build a make-believe playground.

What you can do and say

Invite your child to act out stories such as *The Three Billy Goats Gruff* that use words to describe position and space: *near, inside, outside, far, under, over, next to, between,* and *on top of.* Join in!

This helps your preschool child
Understand and use words that describe position and space.

Describe what your preschool child sees and does:
"Look! You made a square by putting two *triangles* together."
"Aunt Jo's apartment building is *between* the post office and the market."
"You *flipped* the puzzle piece to make it fit."
"You made a playdough ball. What shape are you making now?"
"Let's count the three sides of this *triangle.*"

This helps your preschool child
Learn and use words that tell position and location.
Learn and use shape names and describe shapes.

Encourage your child to work puzzles. Use words like *turn, slide,* or *flip* to help him decide where to put the puzzle pieces.

This helps your preschool child
Learn to move shapes from one direction to another.
Figure out if shapes match.

Invite your child to build towers with blocks. Talk about the blocks that make the best towers and the shapes that do not work well.

This helps your preschool child
Learn how shapes fit together.
Discover features of shapes.

Draw a picture using squares, circles, and triangles. Ask your child to look at it. Then hide the picture and ask your child to draw it from memory. Show your picture again and ask your child to fix his picture if it does not match yours.

This helps your preschool child
Remember shapes.
Draw shapes.

Measurement

- count how many cups of sand it takes to fill a bucket.

- use a piece of ribbon to measure the length of a book.

- walk heel-toe, heel-toe across a room to figure out how many "feet" long the room is.

- say, "I'm more than you – I'm four and a half!"

- run into the kitchen and ask, "When can we eat the cookies?" when she hears the oven timer buzz.

What you can do and say

Talk as you use measurement words. Say, "The store is about 15 miles away. It should take about 20 minutes to get there. We need a rug for the dining room. I think we should buy one that is about 4 feet by 6 feet."

This helps your preschool child
Learn words for measuring.

Describe what your preschool child sees and does:
"You're having trouble picking up that book bag. How *heavy* do you think it is?"
"Are you trying to figure out which one of you is *taller*? Stand back to back with your friend and let's see."
"How much paper do you think we'll need to wrap this birthday present?"

This helps your preschool child
Learn and use words for measuring and estimating.
Learn and use words for comparing.

Model the measuring you do during the day. Talk about how you use measuring tools when you cook, fix things around the house, drive, sew, and so on.

This helps your preschool child
Learn how different tools are used to measure different things.
Learn how measuring is used during daily life.

Invite your child to make good guesses estimates about things like these: "How many cups will fill the bowl?" "How far is it from your bedroom door to the front door?" "How long will it take to clean up your toys?"

This helps your preschool child
Learn and use words that describe estimates.

Patterns and Change

- make up a movement pattern like stomp, clap, clap; stomp, clap, clap; stomp, clap, clap and ask you to follow it.

- see a picture of a milk snake and point out the white, brown; white, brown; white, brown color pattern.

- add new parts to the story, *Brown Bear, Brown Bear, What Do You See?*

- tell his sister, "I'm bigger than you 'cause I growed!"

- look in the gerbil cage and say, "We had two of them, and now we have lots!"

What you can do and say

Point out patterns everywhere. Look for them in clothes, tiles in kitchens, bathrooms, and hallways, books (repeated words or phrases), and behavior. Patterns in behavior include things like everyday routines; clothing worn in different kinds of weather; dancing; or marching.

> **This helps your preschool child**
> Recognize repeated or growing patterns.

Create books with your child about how much she has grown. Suggest book titles, such as *I Was Two but Now I'm Three* or *I Used to Be a Baby, but Now I Am Big!*

> **This helps your preschool child**
> Notice changes that happen in everyday life.

Describe what your preschool child sees and does:
"Help me finish making this quilt. Which shape would fit the pattern?"
"I like the dance step your cousin taught you – step, touch; step, touch; step, slide; step, slide. And you keep repeating the pattern."
"You're right. I always pick you up at school after you've had your afternoon snack."

> **This helps your preschool child**
> Recognize different kinds of patterns.

Invite your child to make patterns with blocks or other toys. Ask her to describe the pattern she has made.

> **This helps your preschool child**
> See, recognize, and repeat relationships that make up patterns.

Collecting and Organizing Information

A preschool child might ...

- sort dolls into two groups: one group with shoes and one without shoes.

- explain how he puts his toy cars away: "My little cars go in the box. The big cars go on the shelf."

- draw a picture of each object that floats and each that sinks after testing them in the bath tub.

- make a graph of a sticker collection, sorting them by color.

- make tally marks under *yes* and *no* on a clipboard to find out if her friends like to drink chocolate milk for snack.

What you can do and say

Ask your child to sort his toys or shoes by color (red and not red) or by size (big and not big). Decide which group has the most objects by matching an object from one group with an object from the other group.

This helps your preschool child
Use two groups to organize information.

Describe what your preschool child sees and does:
"I put your drawings on the cork board. All the pictures about winter are on top and the family pictures are on the bottom."
"I see you made room on the shelf for your new books. You stacked the board books like a tower so that the new books would fit."
"I'm going to bake cupcakes for your birthday party. Let's see how many should have chocolate frosting and how many should have vanilla."

This helps your preschool child
Learn about sorting objects by different features.
Explain why things are in certain groups.
Learn ways to collect information.

Make charts that show family jobs, practice sessions, or homework tasks. Use checks or color coding to show when a job is done.

This helps your preschool child
Learn how information can be shown so that others understand it.

Make a photo album together. Ask your child to tell you which pictures go together. Ask him how the sections should be labeled.

This helps your preschool child
Practice organizing things using his own rules.

Make grocery or other shopping lists together. Organize items by groups, such as cereals, breads, meats, fruit, and so on.

This helps your preschool child
Practice sorting things.
Talk about rule used to sort things into groups.

Your Preschool Child Learns All Day Long

Your preschool child is learning all the time. That's why you can teach your child so many things just by talking about what you see and do together!

Think about all the things you and your child do around the house and when you go out. There are day-to-day routines like getting up and getting dressed, preparing and eating meals, and getting ready to go to bed. There are daily chores like doing the laundry, cleaning the house, and gardening. Math is part of all of them! Each routine and chore gives you and your child a chance to talk and think about numbers, shapes and space, patterns, measuring, and collecting and organizing information.

What math ideas can you point out and talk about when you and your child are taking a walk? At the playground? Riding in a car, on a subway, or on a bus? What about shopping at a hardware or grocery store? These are all great times to ask problem-solving questions, point out math ideas, and use math language.

And don't forget make-believe play! Many preschool children like to play school, dress up with mom's or dad's clothes and shoes and go to work, or make believe they are on a boat or rocket ship. Some like setting up a gas station for cars. Others like to pretend they are shopping or going to a restaurant. When children make believe, they are building important thinking and language skills. These skills are important for math learning as well as learning to read. Think of ways you can add math to your child's make-believe play. For example, catalogs, old charge cards and store receipts, maps, and bus or subway schedules can help your child think about numbers, quantity, space and location, and time as he plays.

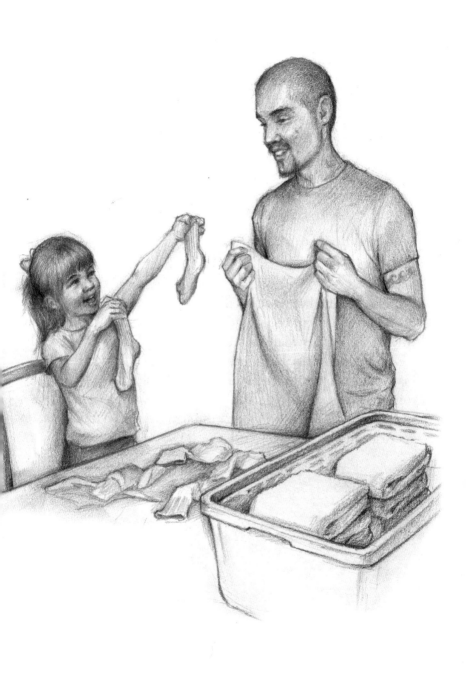

Ready for Kindergarten

All the math talk and math play you have done has given your child a good start on learning math. By now, your child knows a lot about numbers and counting. He can figure out how many things are in a group, and compare groups to see which ones have more or fewer (less). He can identify and name numbers, and maybe even write some! He knows about shapes, size, space, position, direction, and movement. He can compare and figure out things like how long or short something is or if something is heavy or light. He can recognize and create patterns. And he is learning to collect and organize information in a way that makes sense and present it so that others understand what it means. That's a lot of math learning!

Hopefully, you've had fun, too, and have learned that math is not as hard as you think. It's all around us and in everything we do. Your efforts to help your child explore the world of math have been good for her and have made your bond with your child stronger. So don't stop now! Your child needs you to continue to use math words when you describe what you see, hear, and do and what your child sees, hears, and does. She needs you to point out how different math ideas connect to each other and to connect new ideas to things she already knows. And she needs lots of chances to solve problems and help with thinking through a question or problem to get to an answer.

Talk With Your Child's Teacher

Show your child's teacher that you care about your child's learning. Ask her what math ideas and skills she is teaching. Find out what areas of math your child enjoys and if there are any areas where he needs more help. Tell the teacher what you already do at home to support your child's math learning and ask what else you can do. Remember: When home and school are connected in helpful and respectful ways, children feel more secure. And when children feel secure, they are more likely to feel confident about themselves as learners.

Stay Involved

Children who are successful in school usually have family members who follow their progress closely. Make sure your child knows that you think school and learning are important. Get to know your child's teacher. Visit your child's classroom, if possible. If you can, offer to help out in the classroom so you can see for yourself what happens. Know about homework and look at your child's work. If you have questions about the homework, talk to the teacher.

Most of all enjoy just being with your child. Play games, cuddle up and read books, talk about what, how, why, and how many, and enjoy the learning process. Math is fun!

Books to Read With Your Child

Reading and sharing books is a great way to bond with your child and help him learn about math! Here are suggestions for babies, toddlers, and preschool children to help you get started. Talk to your librarian, child care provider, or teacher for even more ideas.

Infants

Numbers

123 bebé/Baby 123 by DK Publishing

Ten Tiny Tickles by Karen Katz

Roll Over! A Counting Song by Merle Peek

Where's the Baby? by Cheryl Christian

Geometry

Black on White by Tana Hoban

White on Black by Tana Hoban

Where Is Baby's Belly Button? by Karen Katz

Baby Dance by Ann Taylor

Patterns

Read Aloud Rhymes for the Very Young by Jack Prelutsky

My Very First Mother Goose illustrated by Rosemary Wells

The Baby Goes Beep by Rebecca O'Connell

Baby Day by Nancy Elizabeth Wallace

Sorting and classifying

That's Not My Teddy by Fiona Watt

Where Is My Baby? By Harriet Zeifert

Toddlers

Numbers

Ten, Nine, Eight by Molly Bang

Toddler Two by Anastasia Suen

My Numbers/Mis numeros by Rebecca Emberley

Mouse Count by Ellen Stoll Walsh

Big Fat Hen by Keith Baker

Geometry

My Shapes/Mis formas/ by Rebecca Emberley

So Many Circles, So Many Squares by Tana Hoban

What Shape? By Debbie MacKinnon

Patterns

I Went Walking by Sue Williams

Brown Bear, Brown Bear, What Do You See? by Bill Martin, Jr.

Is it Time? by Marilyn Janovitz

Sorting and classifying

Of Colors and Things by Tana Hoban

Some Things Go Together by Charlotte Zolotow

Preschool Children

Numbers

More, Fewer, Less by Tana Hoban

Feast for 10 by Cathryn Falwell

Counting with Apollo by Caroline Grégoire

Five Little Monkeys Jumping on the Bed by Eileen Christelow

One Some Many by Marthe Jocelyn

Geometry

Shapes, Shapes, Shapes by Tana Hoban

My Very First Book of Shapes by Eric Carle

Bear in a Square by Stella Blackstone

Apollo by Caroline Grégoire

Elephants Aloft by Kathi Appelt

Measurement

10 Minutes to Bedtime by Peggy Rathmann

The Grouchy Lady Bug by Eric Carle

Tell Me How Much It Weighs (Whiz Kids) by Shirley Willis

Inch by Inch by Leo Lionni

How Big is a Foot? By Rolf Myller

Patterns and Change

Dots, Spots, Speckles and Stripes by Tana Hoban

The Very Hungry Catepillar by Eric Carle

The Doorbell Rang by Pat Hutchins

When I Was Little: A Four-Year-Old's Memoir of Her Youth by Jamie Lee Curtis

My Little Sister Ate One Hare by Bill Grossman

Collecting and Organizing Information

Is It Rough? Is It Smooth? Is It Shiny? by Tana Hoban

Ten Puppies by Lynn Reiser

The Button Box by Margarette Reid

Five Creatures by Emily Jenkins